FULL CIRCLE

Okuhle Esethu

OE PUBLICATIONS

First published in South Africa in 2023 by

OE Publications

ISBN 978-0-6397-8385-7

For more information visit: www.oepublications.com

BOOK OF LOVE

The love you are looking for

is already

within you

CONTENTS

Part 1: Is This Love?

Searching…

Love

Love is a performance.
A senseless act of surrendering
Yourself and your entire existence
To love.

- A prisoner.

Falling

Falling in love is
An act of beating the truth out of
your soul.
Moulding sincerity and gentleness
from your heart.
Tracing kindness from the rims of
your skin.

Falling in love is
A delicate act of balancing
childish carelessness and rationality.
The expression of attraction
liberates and suffocates you.

Loving in my generation

Loving

in my generation is foolish,

an act only committed by demented souls

who numb their senses

and heighten their emotions.

Love

is a default setting for bored human beings.

Those who love soak themselves in elation and gloom,

constantly riding a roller-coaster of tingling exhilaration

and dejected misery, defenseless against suffering.

Loving

in my generation is a thrill

when the passion still burns bright

but leaves one with the bitter taste of

rejection and disappointment in the end.

Burst your heart open

Burst your heart open and let others in!

Yes, you did this before, and life unfaithfully exposed you to treachery. Your heart was tormented, left bleeding and in shards, but everything is worth a second chance. Besides, what is life without love? What is the point of living without a heart that loves? A heart that gets broken and mends itself. A heart that does not cling to old, used-up, and abusive love. A heart that gives love innumerable chances. A heart that loves love and loves with passion. A heart that dares to fall out of the ordinary, familiar, and comfortable, and fall blindly into love's arms. A heart that lets go of what once was and welcomes new love, new experiences, and new people openly. A heart that always does what it is supposed to do—love!

A vulnerable heart

Intimacy is where we reveal ourselves the most,
or try not to reveal ourselves.
Terrified to put our hearts on display,
yet longing to connect.

We build walls around our hearts
and form fortresses to protect ourselves
because someone can destroy us
with the revelation of who we are.

Ur dream girl

to my suitor,

i prefer white roses and handwritten notes.

although i like vines,

i don't drink wine.

i have two left feet

and standards losers can't meet.

i don't intend to be mean,

i still have old messes to clean.

i am not easily pleased,

but my heart is ready to be leased.

Short sprouts of love

Do not drag on a romantic night

with your budding lover into a new day.

Separate when your newly lit fire still burns bright,

so you can have thoughts of them to keep you up at night.

Go home when your chemistry is still untainted

by reality and the scarlet sins of your past,

so the promise of your future together may last.

Dates should end when dates end,

or you risk turning a magical, starry night

into a bitter memory.

Time sucks the sweetness

out of memorable experiences.

Go home after the date,

or you risk learning the true nature

of your new lover too soon.

You risk not getting blindly swept off your feet.

Go home while you are still blinded by infatuation.

A visitor

When love comes your way,

embrace it, appreciate it, enjoy it.

Love every moment of it.

Rejoice in it, bask in the feeling.

Tell the stars, the sun, the moon,

rivers, birds, mountains,

and anyone who cares to listen about it.

When love comes your way,

don't hold back.

Love love back.

Love like there's no tomorrow.

Love like there are no second chances at love.

Hold me

hold me

the way u hold that blunt.

licking its rims

savouring it with ur eyes closed

worshipping it with ur lips

pausing for breath after each puff

purifying urself with it

seeking comfort, warmth and love from it.

i want to be held like that.

Our vow

we lay in silence,

in the thick of the night.

our breaths flowed in the same rhythm.

our hearts danced to the same beat.

both of us yearned to be dancing in one another's garden,

yet neither of us was brave enough to let the other in.

as the moon circled the shy sky,

the air in my bedroom grew dense,

like the tension between us,

with no knife to cut it.

the snake that deceived Eve

rolled between my thighs,

flowed around my waist

and caressed my breast.

yet,

my apple remained unbitten

when we woke up the next morning.

our vow

to wait

until we were "in love"

was stronger than our impulses.

Okuhle Esethu

i like it here

i like it here—

in ur arms,

in the clouds of ur breath,

under u,

on top of u,

next to u.

i like it here.

with u,

i feel safe and seen.

i am valued.

i can freely be myself,

reveal my true nature

and not feel like i am losing parts of myself.

i want to stay here for longer.

i like it here.

Sunflower

i will plant flowers and trees in my heart

so u can live there forever,

not as a friend or a passing lover

but as my forever.

although ur hands are coarse

and ur heart is protected by walls,

i will trust u with my garden

and help with the pruning.

like a sunflower,

my affection may be dormant in winter,

but i bloom with love

when i am loved right.

Okuhle Esethu

Welcoming a new version of love

Love is about introducing yourself
to different versions of love
until you find the best version to pour yourself into.

when flowers bloom more than they wilt,
know that they are being loved right.

i've found my gardener.
in his presence,
with his gentle touch,
my bosom blooms into an erotic tulip,
leaving me with no liberty over our new romance.

he makes love to me
to get a glimpse of my innocence
while giving my body nuance,
redefining what love looks like,
sending me into a terrain of trance-like ecstasy
until i wilt in my skin.

deflowered,

my flower betrays my sobriety.

it cries in desperation for him

to water it then deflower it.

water it and deflower it

again.

    —   an orchestrated dance of love

          performed by blossoming lovers.

my body yearns for him when he is far.

it hushes in his warm embrace.

i flourish in his affection.

his love feels like summer in the middle of winter.

Okuhle Esethu

Writing a love poem

i want to write a love poem with u—
wrap my legs around ur words
while our lips write our love story
and we gasp for air under the sheets of poetry,
running out of breath from creating magic.

if love had a sound,
it would be the sound of our moans
when we climax to each other's poems.

u & i

Okuhle Esethu

Planting seeds of love

we stayed up late to explore

the depths and limits of our bodies.

our souls tied into what felt like eternity.

the starry night was pierced by

our trumpet moans and giggles.

      "u did not take anything from me, my love.

      u gave me a new life and introduced me

      to unfamiliar worlds

      while locating the heaven between my thighs."

planting himself inside me

brushing his lips against mine

bending and reshaping my body

denting the purity of my nature

deflowering me

casting light spells inside my tubes,

he left remnants of our raging love torrents inside me.

Full Circle

our nocturnal activities turned my body into

an explosive cocktail of obsession, lust and swift love.

i satisfied his whims.

his seed now grows inside me.

i tell him this.

he flees like the wind.

My lover is a wind

My lover is a wind.

A wind that fleets.

He does not stay in one place.

On a brutally cold and starry winter night,

the world blows him in my direction.

He finds me lonesome and lost,

and sweeps me off my feet.

He rescues me from loneliness,

briefly shelters me with conditional affection,

then leaves when i am out of breath,

desperate for his love.

He refuses to make a home out of my love.

"A man can only love a woman briefly, in the beginning.

Once she loves him back,

he must leave and travel to other worlds.

A man is a wind."

He says.

Is this love?

we only fell in love
when we imagined ourselves making love.
u only loved me when i invited u inside me.
i only loved u when i had my legs open for u
and u were hyperventilating
like u would take ur last breath on top of me.

i only kissed u when i imagined his soft lips
gently touching against mine.
i allowed u to cup my youthful breasts
and caress my butt
because it felt like ur hands were his.

Only looks like love

You do not love yourself.

You do not see yourself.

You do not respect yourself

You do not think you are worthy of love.

So, you settle for what only looks like love.

Temporary pleasure
Long-lasting pain

we kissed,
and u planted ur presence inside me.
it drowned my sorrows and silenced my demons.
i watched, delighted,
as the sun and the moon swelled with envy
when my lips gently touched urs.

ur embrace dissolved all my problems
and made me feel like i had the riddles of life
figured out.
but our encounter has been
temporary pleasure and long-lasting pain.

i confused ur lust for love.
my mistake was falling in love
with the idea of being in love with u
instead of falling in love with u.

Okuhle Esethu

i was rash, reckless and irrational.

the spirit of love divorced from rationality

is unprogressive and destructive.

ur face was incomparable,

ur body so glorious,

ur mind even more captivating.

u were everything i once dreamt of,

but u left me with wounds that now resemble

dead lust and infatuation.

Worlds apart

In the red venom skies,

ur face subsides,

and our love dies.

We are here because of ur lies.

Okuhle Esethu

A stranger with a familiar face

we had a date with destiny.

the fate of our paths crossing

was written in the stars.

but i have buried the desire to be with u

with all ur lies,

behind those red venom skies.

u left without fulfilling ur promises.

each day renders me free

from my blind love for u.

every minute distorts the memories i have of u.

like an old woman with amnesia,

i think i will look at u someday

and not recognize u,

but mistaken u for a man i once loved.

Full Circle

my muscles will spasm,

my heartbeat will quicken,

my buried anxiety will resurface,

when i glance in ur direction,

trace familiarity from ur face,

but not know which world i know u from.

Okuhle Esethu

Building a love castle

i built a sandcastle

for us,

as a symbol of our love,

but a wave came and swept it away.

i built a home

for us,

made of cards,

but the wind came and blew it away.

i built a shelter of love, under the red venom sky,

for us,

from sticks and candles,

but it torched itself down.

i cannot build this love castle alone.

You wanted a fire to keep you warm.

You sought out love and found him.

The cold winters bit through the skin of your heart and
froze your fingers and toes before him.

His love was warm and safe until it grew into a wildfire
that threatened to burn you.

You know you have to walk away, or you risk dying in his
forest flame of love.

But you choose to stay because you are human;
human beings tend to gravitate towards the familiar.

That is what love looks like when you are scarred
and unhealed.

You do not think you have the strength or spark inside you
to walk away and kindle a new flame.

Even if you did, you suppose it would drain you and
demand too much of your energy, because newness
requires one to renew herself.

You will have to revisit the woods, get lost and confused,
put yourself out there, open yourself up to a new world
and new people, stumble and fall, again! before finding
the right kind of flame for you.

Okuhle Esethu

All of that seems more daunting and dangerous than
tolerating his fire, which burns you every evening.
So, you stay, hoping that his love will dwindle back to the
safe, gentle and kind fire you once knew.
Although his love is brutal and burns your self-image to
ashes of self-loathe, at least you still have love,
you convince yourself.

Black Love

bored with the banality of my existence,

my heart had to bear the burden of my ethnicity.

i've tried to escape myself by loving men.

i've searched for myself in the faces of men,

in the traces of their skin,

in their glossy eyes,

and grim hands.

i drowned in their ocean tongues,

swept off my feet by their waves of lies,

and swallowed up by their traumatic histories.

desperate to be loved by men

who could not love themselves,

i risked making my heart

a prison,

myself

the prisoner.

i lost myself

trying to occupy the intricate minds and hearts of men

who were too occupied trying to escape

their sooty skins and bruised existence,

to make time to learn

how love holds a woman,

speaks to her,

loves her,

and makes love to her.

we

did not have the leisure of loving freely.

love is free,

but our mothers' breasts did not lactate freedom.

we sucked on fear and anticipated anxiety.

our fathers exhaled abuse and abandonment

into the air.

we inhaled that and called it

love!

black love.

that is how a black man loves.

we

held onto that love

even though it killed us.

some of us.

most of us.

all of us.

it was all we knew.

we

became desperate prisoners,

wanting to be loved by everything around us

but us,

by the world that made our existence banal,

by pale gods,

by the land our ancestors hoed,

by the oceans they drowned in,

by those who did not see us,

by those who were like us,

searching for themselves and love

in familiar places and people,

in perpetually traumatic histories.

Okuhle Esethu

we

were imprisoned from within.

we

found nothing worth loving within.

before learning to love,

before welcoming love,

we

had to escape ourselves first

and redefine love.

The birth of misogyny

Men are born innocent, pure

and filled with love.

No one is born a sinner.

U must have learned

how to hate a woman

when u sucked on ur mother's breasts

as she lactated fear and self-hate,

planted inside her by ur father.

U must have discovered

this misogyny

from ur frail father's fables of his boyhood.

U must have been taught

these destructive ways of being a man

by the shadows of ur father's menacing voice

when he played tug of war

with his masculinity and emotionality.

Part 2: Love Hangover.

Hurting…

Little girl

Little girl dreamed.

Little girl dreamed of her Cinderella fairytale.

Little girl could only dream of a life with
Prince Charming.

Little girl romanticised Prince Charming.

Little girl wasted her youth waiting for Prince Charming.

One day,

Little girl's dream came true, but Prince Charming
was a nightmare.

Little girl fell in love with Prince Charming
and discovered that he was a brute.

Okuhle Esethu

Little girl tried to fit herself into Cinderella's
slippers to charm Prince Charming.

Little girl grew self-hate on her toes in Cinderella's
glass slippers.

Little girl loved Prince Charming,
but he had no love in him, even for himself.

Little girl wanted to leave but believed Prince Charming
was her only home.

Little girl broke herself trying to fix Prince Charming.

We lost little girl when we told her to worship
Prince Charming.

We should have taught little girl how to love herself.

Little girl made of glass

the sun rises,

shining a little brighter today,

only to find her spirit shattered

and her heart in shards.

this will be her form for a while

until she finds herself again.

little girl made of glass,

too fragile for frail men.

erased in the stardust of memory by her own thoughts.

an unknown element to herself.

non-existent in her own world.

swept away by the winds of betrayal.

Okuhle Esethu

Betrayal

i woke up this morning
wishing it was all a dream:
my swelled heart,
his unfaithfulness,
our broken trust.

however,
the stinging memory of his treachery
lingered long enough to correct my ignorance.
its vividness exaggerated his indifference.

i woke up this morning
with the remnants of a scarring dream
carried over from our bitter reality.

my head pounded from
the hangover of our short-lived affair.
the edges of my lips were encrusted with
the lies his kisses told.

Full Circle

our love was a passing thing.

his affection was a performance.

i was the enthusiastic clown.

Okuhle Esethu

Dwelling

when u kissed me goodbye,

after planting seeds of love in my heart,

i revisited the past.

when u left,

after begging me to stay and water ur garden,

i built a dwelling in our past.

when u plucked me from ur heart,

the way a gardener plucks weeds from his garden,

i wasted precious time dwelling on

when our promising romance began to decay.

Love letter

this letter gives visible form to my wildest fears.

i am bloated with shame now that i have written it.

i have recorded my feelings for u on it.

i have revealed my weaknesses;

exposed the workings

of my senseless mind and desperate heart.

u might think of me as a fool now,

but unconfessed feelings are better off on paper

than in the heart.

u have become a distant dream to me,

a manifestation of mild, impossible romances.

u are only a fantasy residing at the periphery

of my imagination.

so, have this love letter and return my heart.

Our last kiss

Had i known that i'd be kissing u for the last time,
the last time i kissed u,
i would have kissed u with endless passion.
i would have held onto ur body for life
while weeping in the warmth of ur kiss
and ur cold goodbye.

Had i known that i'd be kissing u for the last time,
the last time i kissed u,
i would have taken u home with me.
i would have sneaked u into my eternity
and dug my nails into ur skin
to mark my presence
and leave remnants of myself
and our love on ur body.

Had i known that i'd be kissing u for the last time,
the last time i kissed u,
i would have invited u inside me with

Full Circle

a desperate and aroused heart.

i would have moaned in love's voice

so my neighbours heard that i came an inch close

to experiencing love that makes one feel alive.

i would have begged u to plant seeds of urself inside me

so i could have parts of u even when u are long gone.

Had i known that i'd be kissing u for the last time,

the last time i kissed u,

i would have kissed u like i did not want to let u go.

Okuhle Esethu

Old flames

Old flames are like forest fires.

If you do not put them out,

they burn themselves out,

after burning you.

Full Circle

Do not drag on a romance for longer than it wishes to last,

or else the sweet experience of it will lose its

splendour and flavour, leaving you with a bitter memory.

It will turn your passionate love for your lover

into noxious hate that dents

the pure and magical memories of the love

you once shared.

Old flames are like forest fires.

If you do not put them out,

they burn themselves out,

after burning you.

So tragic is a dead romance.

More horrific, however, is a dead romance

that leaves one disapproving of love and full of hate.

Do not hold onto dead things,

leave when there's still love.

Grief

i was 10

the first time i mourned.

i never imagined i'd mourn a living human being at 20.

ur departure was death camouflaged as a breakup.

ur departure,

death's fellow,

was ruthless.

it tore my heart into a collection of unrecognisable

pieces of myself

that seemed impossible to reassemble.

ur departure,

a careless goodbye,

bruised my ego.

it plunged me into a dark hole,

where the bereaved gather

to nurse their wounds.

Full Circle

"the first cut is always the deepest."

this is my second cut,

deeper than the first.

an abyss of agony.

i am attempting to get over

how miraculous our love once was.

i don't know if time will heal this wound.

all it does is cheat me of my memories of u.

they grow vague with each day that passes,

just like ur face in my mind.

is that what healing looks like?

feeling and remembering the pain

but forgetting the inflictor of it.

i've buried recollections of u

with all the unwanted emotions, like grief,

because ur existence,

away from me,

is a denial

of love and life.

Emotions

Bury me with all these unwanted emotions.
A part of me died when u left.

The world is dull and motionless
without u.

The tension between what
i feel and think is agonizing.

Resisting wanting u while loathing u
is more excruciating than mourning death.

Not with u

although i am not with u,

i cannot dream of a life

where i am not in love with u.

even though we are separated

by distance, circumstances,

old wounds, and our egos,

i still want to love u.

i want lay in ur arms

while u share ur dreams

and visions of the future with me.

i want ur lips to touch mine

and feel one with u.

i am not urs;

u are not mine,

but i cannot dream of a life without u.

Okuhle Esethu

What once was

i was once
cloaked by ur love;
i felt safe with u.

the day u chose me,
the sky became my home;
i felt like i could fly.

i am now
choked by a familiar feeling from my past—
overwhelming displacement.

Full Circle

What do you do when he has shut his door?

You ask.

He slammed it in your face and refuses to reopen it.

You've wailed a puddle into an ocean for him to come
back to you. You begged him to open the door to his heart
again so you could rewrite your love story.

You screeched at the heavens and questioned God
until your throat burned like hot coal when you lost him
to her. You violently hurled insults at both of them,
mostly her. You desperately scratched and banged
his door night after night for him to let you back in.

You threatened to turn yourself into a violent storm
that would disturb their peace.

You tried to perfect yourself for him.

You begged for forgiveness even though you were not in
the wrong. You recounted all that you had done for him
and sacrificed to make it work.

And despite all of that, he still chooses her over you.

You gave up chunks of yourself to prove your love and
loyalty. That was all in vain. It means nothing to him.

You cannot bully your way into love.

You have to walk away.

Lust

i've known love.

i've tasted lust,

gotten a glimpse of it

and confused it for love.

i've been desperate to mould

lust into

never-ending, deep, passionate, and sincere love.

i've lived a lie.

lust and love

are not even cousins.

love stays.

lust is a vagabond.

u've found urself a new home,

yet again.

i am still where

u found and left me.

Vanity

i've   lost   u

In this sea of ghostly human beings.

A stormy body of water that believes

Love is not real.

Yet

Worships everything shallow.

Swallow... Swallow...

Their lies

And see how hollow ur heart becomes.

An empty cup

With no one to pour love into it.

Okuhle Esethu

Dementia

the first signs of dementia manifest
as i...

                   forget

                            forget myself

       forget how to love myself

          forget what love looks like

forget how my parents loved me

            forget that i deserve love

       forget how a man is supposed to love his woman

forget that a woman is not supposed to love a man
with no love

          forget that love is not enough

Remember

Do you remember?

Before it all slipped away from you—

His gentleness

The love you shared

Yourself

Do you remember?

Your life

Before him

Before it all slipped away from you...

Do you remember?

When he ceased being a man

And it all slipped away from you—

Your dignity

The love you had for yourself

It all slipped away from you...

You lost yourself loving a violent brute.

Remembering

u left...

now i have to remind myself of what life was like

before u.

i have to go back to my past and remind myself

that i am whole and worthy,

even when u do not choose me.

i have to bury our past

and stop romanticizing our lifeless love.

the mountains of feelings that weigh heavily on my body

make forgetting harder than i think it should be—

indescribable love. longing. deep sadness.

hatred. disgust. self-pity. emptiness.

loss. disappointment. confusion.

raging rage. frustration.

Full Circle

ur departure evoked emotions

i never knew existed.

i dreamt of a forever with u.

i conjured up cliché fantasies—

cinderella and her prince charming.

u left...

now i have to try to move on

while mourning what could have been.

Okuhle Esethu

Monument

She who never forgets.

This place has become u
and a shadow of our love.
It has dead romance written all over its walls.

My heart aches as i glide past the halls,
knowing that our fantasy will never be re-lived.
Every glass door and window reflects
old memories of us.

U've slipped away from the clasp of my hands
into the arms of another woman.
Now all i have to hold onto are old memories of us,
with this place as a monument of our dead love.

Forgetting

Forgetting is work.

You have to make yourself

do a lot more things

so you don't have time to remember.

Your life was so deeply intertwined with his.

He was your morning cup of coffee, your lunch, and your dinner. He was your favourite hobby; the only thing that brought you joy. He was a part of everything that you did, a part of every moment of your life, even when he was not there. You couldn't enjoy life when he was not around, you didn't allow yourself to. He populated your thoughts and blew up your phone. You stopped nurturing dear friendships because he was the centre of your life. You stopped doing the things you loved; he became your only love. He was all that mattered in your world. He liked you and you loved him, dearly! But now he is gone. The flame that once kept you warm has died out. You have to go on without him. You have to learn to live again. You have to learn to love yourself through this loss and heartache. The next time you decide to love, love wholeheartedly, but do not lose yourself in love.

The next time i fall in love

The next time i fall in love,

i shall be charming yet cunning like a horse.

i will have my guard up and trust my intuition.

i will be cautious of the flags that glow and glare in red.

Only sacred hands shall touch my tainted body,

hands layered with safety and gentleness.

The next time i fall in love,

i shall be calm yet deadly like the rain.

i will bring peace to those that love me.

i will give life when i am loved right,

but claim lives when my heart is brutalized,

by bringing floods to the surface of the earth.

Love-bombing

This is how it goes:

A terrorist walks into your life cloaked as a knight.

Saves you from the misery of loneliness.

Offers you heaven.

Makes you float in the clouds for a while.

Reels you in with irresistible affection

Until you give him attention.

As soon as you give in,

Love him back,

He pulls back,

Plunging you into a deeper trench of misery.

Leaving your spirit shattered

By the explosion of a failed fantasy.

Picked from a garden

Yesterday, i finally gave up.

Not on my fantasy.

Not on that boy.

Not on the promise of our love.

i gave up trying to be

a cannibal plant

when i was meant to be

a rose.

He will love me.

He will love me as i am,

with my sharp thorns and beautiful yet delicate petals,

if he wishes to.

Okuhle Esethu

Ur love

i don't want love
that comes in bits and pieces.
love that sings my body praise today
and tears my heart into tatters the next.

i don't want love
that is seasonal—
cold like winter, only warm in summer,
blooms in secret in spring, when no one is watching.

i don't want love
that is dense with doubt and insecurity.
love that makes me love life with u
while loathing myself and my love for u.

i love u, but i don't want ur love anymore.

The last time i cried for u

The last time i cried for u,

i felt that i would be crying for u

for the last time.

i curled up in bed

with my heart hunched in pain

and wailed so i would cease being vain.

The last time i cried for u,

i did not cry because i longed for ur love.

i cried to erase u from memory.

The last time i cried for u,

i knew that i would never cry for u again;

my tears drowned our fatal fantasy.

Okuhle Esethu

Broken things

u wanted to be healed, not loved.

u convinced me to open up so u could show me love.

i opened the emotionally secured gates to my heart for u

even though my intuition whispered to me

that u were a broken man.

i was desperate for anything that looked like love.

so, i silenced a voice that was love.

u helped me break down the walls

i had built around my heart

then wrecked my heart once u were inside.

i assumed that by loving u

in ways i had never loved myself,

i could repair what was broken in u before me

to avoid fixing what was broken in me before u.

we were each other's rebounds,

bounded by traumas we did not want to heal.

rebounds are like match-stick flames,

they burn out hastily

and always burn the person trying too hard

to keep the relationship together.

we did not need each other.

we had no love to give one another.

we needed space and time alone,

to heal and find ourselves.

damaged egos require long healing periods,

not short sprouts of love.

my heart and ur mood swings

played tug of war

because of our fragile egos and brutalized pasts.

i broke my own heart trying to love u.

u left when u thought u had won

but lost parts of urself in our war.

by trying to love u when u were not ready for love,

i carried the burden of ur past.

i suffered the sins of those who hurt u in the past.

a fire now burns in my heart,

for i have burnt my flesh and bones to keep u warm

and to catch a glimpse of ur mysterious heart.

the light that shone in the darkness of our lovemaking

revealed the workings of ur broken spirit.

like u,

i was broken,

with a past and emotional wounds to heal.

but, loving myself was harder than loving u.

trying to fix what is broken in others is easier

than fixing a mirror to myself

and looking for the broken fragments of myself.

one cannot build a congregation out of mirrors,

but we can always worship someone else,

love them to escape ourselves.

breaking my heart was ur default setting.

my heartbreak was a response to trauma.

we were broken spirits

with blood and desperation

smeared all over the chambers of our hearts.

Full Circle

ur heart was never mine.

i lost myself in the mess u called ur past

trying to heal u.

a voice whispered to me the day u left,

"Okuhle, you are a lover, not a healer.

stop trying to fix what you did not break!"

Gentleness

You get over a heartbreak

By not trying to get over it.

You need to just let the sadness linger in your heart.

Don't label it.

Don't judge it,

Or yourself for feeling it.

Let the pain loom over you until it grows numb.

Until it grows tired of hurting you

And eventually redirects you towards healing.

The agony won't magically or rapidly fizzle into

Nothingness.

You won't suddenly forget about it,

And how heavy it is.

But it will grow into wisdom,

A light that guides you to a better you.

Healing comes after you have allowed yourself to

Feel all your emotions:

Full Circle

Anger. Sadness. Frustration.

Shame. Heaviness. Confusion.

Loss. Fear. Loneliness. Desperation.

Emptiness. Brokenness. Etc. Etc. Etc.

You get over a heartbreak

When you stop trying to get over it.

You never win by fighting your own emotions.

Okuhle Esethu

Redirection

when i finally accepted it.

i no longer felt sad or angry.

i was awakened.

u conjured up old, buried emotions.

u triggered ancient wounds

and redirected me towards healing.

thank u!

Part 3: Stumbling Upon Love.

Discovering…

YOU

Little girl

Little girl.

Who taught you to romanticize romantic relationships so much that you don't even dream of, live, or create a life for yourself outside of them?

Who told you that men are the prize and you are not worthy or good enough unless they pick you?

Who taught you to not look in the mirror for validation but to men who hate you and don't even love themselves?

Who told you to never be merry alone but to yearn so desperately to be married?

Who taught you about love but never pointed you to the love that comes from within?

Who told you that safety can only be found in the arms of a man, in his embrace and words, not inside your heart and in solitude?

Who taught you to look for love outside yourself before even building a home within yourself?

Who deceived you and made you a prisoner of love that is not even genuine but flees like the wind and torments your soul?

Who planted those seeds of self-hate inside you and grew a garden of a pathetically desperate and dependent woman, who doesn't even know who she is?

Okuhle Esethu

Familiar feelings

The day he decided to part,
my world fell apart.
I bawled at the heavens.
A gloomy cloud of loneliness
mixed with deep sadness
hovered over my grieving body.
I blamed him and everybody.

When I grew tired of labelling him
as the source of my unhappiness,
I traced back my steps
to get to the real cause of my emptiness.
I dug up buried emotions and deeply entrenched beliefs
to measure the depth of my brokenness.
I conjured up ancient memories of my ghostly exes
to inspect where I had gone wrong each time.

With time,
I realized that they all left eventually.

Full Circle

They left in different ways,

at different times in our love journey,

yet their departures aroused familiar feelings

inside me every time.

The day he left,

I cried.

I cursed the heavens, and him,

for making me feel what I felt

until I realized that those feelings

resembled my past.

They were familiar feelings.

Too familiar.

Like a house I had lived in before.

Like a mirror pointed to old wounds

I had expected my old lovers and him to take care of.

The day he left,

I learned that he was not responsible for how I felt,

I was.

So, I began to take care of the wounds that plagued

my heart and soul.

Bare

Bare.

Skin and limbs in tatters.

Heart and spirit in shards.

Bare woman dancing on the eggshells of broken men

while their slurs echo the whispers of misogyny.

Mold

In disgust,
I watch as the walls of my fortress bulge
like wet wood.

One stench!
and the vultures of self-pity have circled me,
attracted by the smell of ruin coming from my body.

It's the rain!
The rain turned this fortress into a body of mold.
"How does one mould herself out of ruin, mother?"

Okuhle Esethu

Home

She knew!

She felt it in her core.

Her body was healing.

The heart transforming itself.

She wrote less poems about him.

She ceased scrambling desperately for his love

in stanzas and his puns.

She became her own home and searched for love within.

She began to write about herself.

Her love for who she was becoming grew

into an errant ray of sunshine on a cloudy day.

Songs of boundless joy filled her soul.

You will never be at peace as long as your home is someone else. Create a home within yourself so you can always have yourself to return to. You will get lost in this maze of love. You will lose yourself while trying to build altars of love with others. Therefore, it is wise to always have yourself to return to when a connection with another human being dwindles and dies. When you are your own home, you return to yourself to look for love, healing and forgiveness—not other human beings—when your heart gets broken and you are fraught with agony. When you have created a home within yourself, you do not waste your precious life hopscotching from relationship to relationship, house to house, person to person, looking for love and happiness. You love yourself, and your home is you. So, even when your lovers become fickle and decide to flee, you still feel safe. Even when you are rejected by those you love, you still feel loved, because you are your first love.

Solitude

Long periods of solitude and silence

become necessary when all you've known is chaos,

and the outside noise drowns the whispers from within.

Seek peace!

Your soul starves for YOUR love.

Stardust

Skin swelled with sorrow.

    *self—a stardust in a galaxy of suffering.

Swimming in a shallow swamp of sorries.

Shadows of my senseless past haunt me.

So, I'll sit still in this somberness until I am soothed.

Okuhle Esethu

Silence

healing shapes itself as

silence

the noisy thoughts that once gnawed

at the mind quiet down

the chaos that tormented

the soul dissipates

life slows down

making space for a new kind of love

Rain

Drenched in the showers of self-love.

Basking in your own glory.

They thought you lost your sense

when you connected to God through all your senses.

You danced to the tune of your own spirit

while they lost themselves

in the asylum of self-betrayal,

looking for love outside of themselves.

Ocean

My world has become
A peaceful altar.

My body is now
A gentle wave.

My heart has no space
For chaotic souls.

Still

I knew I was healing
when I could just be still.

My heart not tormented
by ravaging emotions.
My mind not wandering
to ancient people, places, and events.

I was just still.
In the moment.
Present within myself.
Appreciating the gracefulness of life.

Okuhle Esethu

Sunset

I was searching for the sunset

when I set my eyes upon

a once battered body

blooming into a flower of wisdom and love.

I was searching for the sunset

when I saw a body

that embraced love

become love.

I was searching for the sunset

when I witnessed a body

become its own

source of love.

I was searching for the sunset

when I gazed upon a body

once burdened by a bruised ego

reflecting the beauty of the sunset as it surrendered to love.

Fleeting wind

I am a fleeting wind.

A summer breeze that no one can apprehend.

A breath of fresh air that no man can seize.

My love has no shape or size.

I can cool men and leave them dry

with no shame when they cry.

My body is a sea that you will never snatch.

It moves in a fast, thrilling beat that no man can catch.

It dances like a wave

and only holds men that are brave.

I am a peace omen.

The gateway to heaven.

I elude loveless men.

Light

You never lost it,
Your inner light.

The storms you've gone through have clouded it.
There are shadows that lurk above it.

It is still there,
Waiting for you to return to your true self.

Search deep within yourself.
Re-torch your inner light.

Waiting

If you spend your life waiting for "the one" to finally be happy, they might eventually come into your life and bring you the happiness you waited so long for. But, you would have wasted some of the best years of your life waiting.

Okuhle Esethu

Healing

Healing is moving from a place of
<u>wanting</u> love to <u>desiring</u> love.

<u>Want</u> is desperate and needy.
It is fears solitude and perceives each day lived in the
absence of a lover as time spent in the pits of misery.
It is a parasite, sucking joy from others because
it doesn't know that true joy can only come from within.
Insecurity drives it to seek security and shelter from
outsiders.

<u>Desire</u> is composed and filled with hope.
It yearns for companionship yet finds contentment
in solitude.
It teaches itself love and heals first before seeking love
from outsiders.
It trusts that what it seeks will come when the time
is right.
It loves love and life, with and without a lover.

Journal

Journaling is

Listening to your soul,

Connecting to your heart,

Getting to know yourself deeply.

It is an act of love that validates

Your EXISTENCE, FEELINGS and EXPERIENCES.

Intimacy

It's all cobwebs and spiders in the basement.

Dust gathering.

Insects crawling.

It aches to be cleaned, the basement.

It longs to be touched again,

by me.

It's not just a single part of the house, this basement.

It's where parts of my sovereign self are stored.

It's what connects me to my femininity and sexuality.

Exploring the Self

At first, you feel weird when you do it.

You feel dirty and vulgar.

Your mind races,

and your conscience paces

as if you were committing a crime.

Our parents and those around us

whisper to us that it is vile to touch ourselves,

to explore the depths and limits of our bodies

before lending them to outsiders.

We are taught to never touch ourselves

as if our bodies do not belong to us.

But which mechanic sells a car without

knowing about its parts?

What homemaker invites visitors into her home

with no clue of where the spoons are kept

and where the secret corridors and corners are?

Okuhle Esethu

How can we discover ourselves
if we never allow ourselves
to trace fingers around the intricacies
of our eternities,
in an effort to learn about
what pleases and pleasures our bodies?

Pleasure is an uncomfortable act
committed more than once.
Our bodies are wonders of the world,
sights for the experience of pleasure
and self-discovery.
Sights that deserve to be seen, loved,
and acknowledged by us.
Sights designed to give form to our fantasies
and expression to our sexualities.

Discover and explore alone first
before inviting outsiders into your home.

Intuition

Self-discovery requires you to pour yourself
into different versions of love
until you find the best version to pour yourself into.
IT IS A PROCESS!
You have to keep loving yourself in different ways,
figuring out what works and what doesn't,
what feels like love and what makes you hate yourself,
until you stumble upon a certain feeling.

A feeling that feels worth holding onto.
A feeling that holds you with care.
A feeling that makes you see you.
A feeling that makes you feel loved and worthy of love.

When you've found the love you deserve—that feeling—
your heart, your body, and your soul will recognize it.
Intuition recognizes what is real and what you deserve.
You will know you've found your best version of love
when you love loving yourself.

Okuhle Esethu

Holding a planet

Fall for the love that loves you back.

Love that holds you the way God holds a planet.

Love that does not make you feel like you are asking

for the whole world when you are only asking

to be loved.

Emotional warmth

You hate the cold.

You like feeling warm.

You like the sun and hearth fires.

You like the warmth that you feel inside you.

"Emotional warmth"

The warmth that feels like you have a blanket covering

your heart.

The warmth that makes you feel loved and valued

by you.

The warmth that makes you feel

like you.

You'd set yourself on fire for this warmth.

You'd burn your bones and skin for it,

because nothing is like it.

Once lit,

it never burns out;

it burns from within.

Suffering

Do not glorify suffering.

You went through it.

It was painful.

You are grateful.

It moulded you into what you are today,

but you did not deserve to go through that.

So, where to from here?

"So, where to from here?" You ask.

One day at a time.

Live again.

Smile.

Cry.

Laugh from the belly.

Dance.

Sing along to your favourite songs.

Romanticize your life.

Dream.

Work hard.

See the world.

Rest.

Go to therapy.

Journal.

Let go of the past.

Be kind to yourself.

Learn and unlearn.

Okuhle Esethu

Try new things.

Make mistakes.

Fail forwards.

Open yourself to the world.

Forgive.

Clean your room.

Buy yourself flowers.

Spoil yourself.

Go on a solo date.

Be creative.

Have fun.

Don't take yourself too seriously.

Rediscover yourself.

Connect to yourself on a deeper level.

Listen to your inner voice.

Trust your intuition.

Stand up straight with your shoulders back.

Fall in love with yourself.

Welcome love.

Love!

Paradise

What humans destroy, art heals.

What humans feel, art expresses.

She was art itself.

        Through her eyes, which led to

           the depths of her soul,

      doses of paradise could be extracted.

Blissfully in love

When her figures of love decided to part,
at first, it felt like her world was falling apart.
She had no idea that she was coming back home,
to herself,
to the fullness of her divinity.
Layers of her delusion and desperation
were falling away in clumps.

The universe was calling to her to return to her soul,
to become her own source of joy, love, and peace.
She heeded the call.
She built herself a kraal of love.
She discovered joy in the traces of her curved smile.

Little girl lived blissfully in love with herself,
within herself.

Full Circle

In search of love,

you step outside of yourself,

wandering into situations and people

that look like love

but are nothing like love,

only to discover that the love

you have been looking for

has always been inside you.

About The Author

Okuhle Esethu, legally known as Lindokuhle Esethu Hlatshwayo, is a South African writer, poet, performer, and literature enthusiast with an undying passion for storytelling. She holds a Bachelor of Arts degree from the University of Johannesburg, where she graduated cum laude, double-majoring in Literature and Film Studies. Her innovative talents were recognized with an award for the most innovative screenplay at the third-year level.